The ABC Book of Feelings

By Kathryn Lescroart Detzer

The ABC Book of Feelings

Written & Illustrated By Kathryn Lescroart Detzer

Copyright © 2015 Kathryn Lescroart Detzer

All rights reserved. No part of this publication may be reproduced in any form without written permission by the author.

Aa

Angry

Bb

Bored

Cc

Curious

Dd

Determined

Ee

Eager

Ff

Friendly

Gg

Guilty

Hh

Happy

Impatient

Jj

Joyful

Kk

Kooky

Love

Mm

Melodramatic

Nn

Nervous

Oo

Ornery

Pp

Peaceful

Rr

Relaxed

Ss

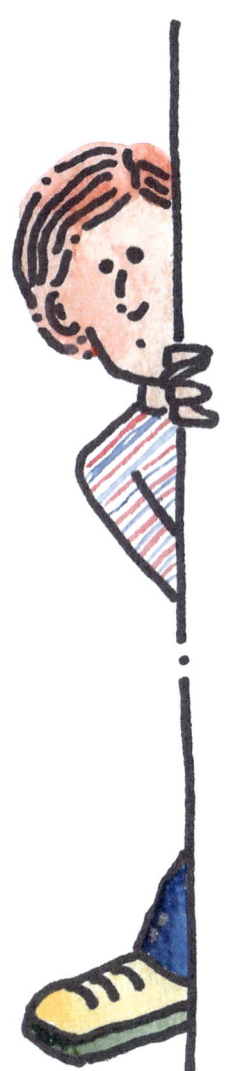

Shy

Tt

Thoughtful

Uu

Unhappy

Vv

Vain

Ww

Wishful

Xx

eXcellent

Yy

Yearning

Zz

Zestful

Acknowledgements

I want to thank my husband, Mark, who has loved and supported me from the first illustration in this book thirty years ago, when I self-published this book in black and white for my nieces and nephews. He sold a family heirloom so that we could afford to have this little book printed, which I consider to be an amazing expression of love and support. I gave copies of this book to friends and family in 1984, many of whom have kept it on their shelves for all these years for which I am grateful.

I am so proud of my creative sons, Noah and Paul, both so supportive and appreciative of my art. You bring my great joy!

Special thanks to Sarah Hudson and Susan Vigsnes for their encouragement and valuable input on layout, illustration and everything in between.

Made in the USA
San Bernardino, CA
07 April 2016